The Human Body
Moving and Eating

First published 2020
Foxton Books
London, UK

Copyright © Foxton Books, 2020

ISBN: 978-1-83925-003-3

Written by Nichola Tyrrell
Designed by Maryke Goldie
Logo design: Stewart Wright (2Wright Design)
Cover design: Ed White
Education consultant: Frances Barlow

About Foxton Primary Science:

The Foxton Primary Science series supports Key Stage 1, Lower Key Stage 2
and Upper Key Stage 2 Science.

This title supports **Lower Key Stage 2** requirements for the *Animals, including humans* content
through a variety of features and **STEAM**-inspired tasks that cover all curriculum requirements.

Colourful, engaging content blends information with prompts
for further discussion and investigation.

Keywords, creative activities and quizzes reinforce comprehension,
along with challenging words (in bold) explained in the glossary.

Contents

Moving and eating

There are many amazing parts that make up the human body. Different body parts have special **functions**, too. They all work together to **enable** us, humans, to survive and grow.

Underneath the skin are bones and muscles that we use to move our body.

Keywords   bones   energy   food   muscles

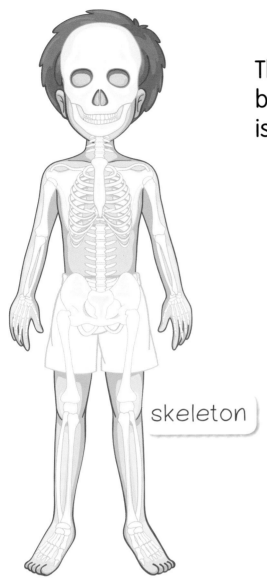

skeleton

The group of bones in the body is a skeleton.

What do you think we might look like if we didn't have bones?

What do you think would happen if we didn't eat any healthy food?

For the human body to work properly, it needs energy and **nutrients**.

We get energy from eating healthy food.

The skeleton

The human skeleton has more than 200 bones! It supports and protects the body and helps it to move. Try feeling your own bones under your skin.

The skull is the bone that protects the **brain**.

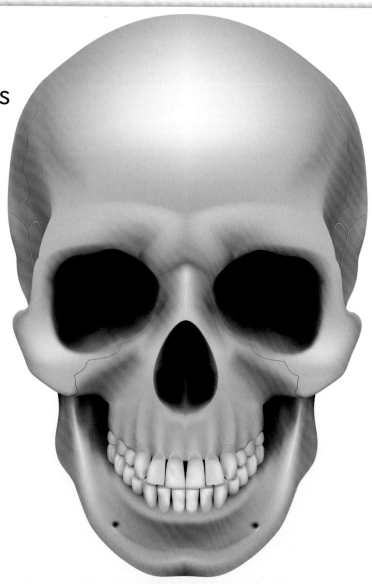

Keywords joints ribs skeleton skull

Ribs are a set of thin bones that curve around the middle of the body to protect the heart and lungs.

The place where two bones meet is a **joint**. The bones are connected with a **ligament tissue**. Joints allow body parts to bend. The knee, ankle, elbow and wrist are all joints.

Trace this skeleton and label the bones. See how many you can label without looking at the book!

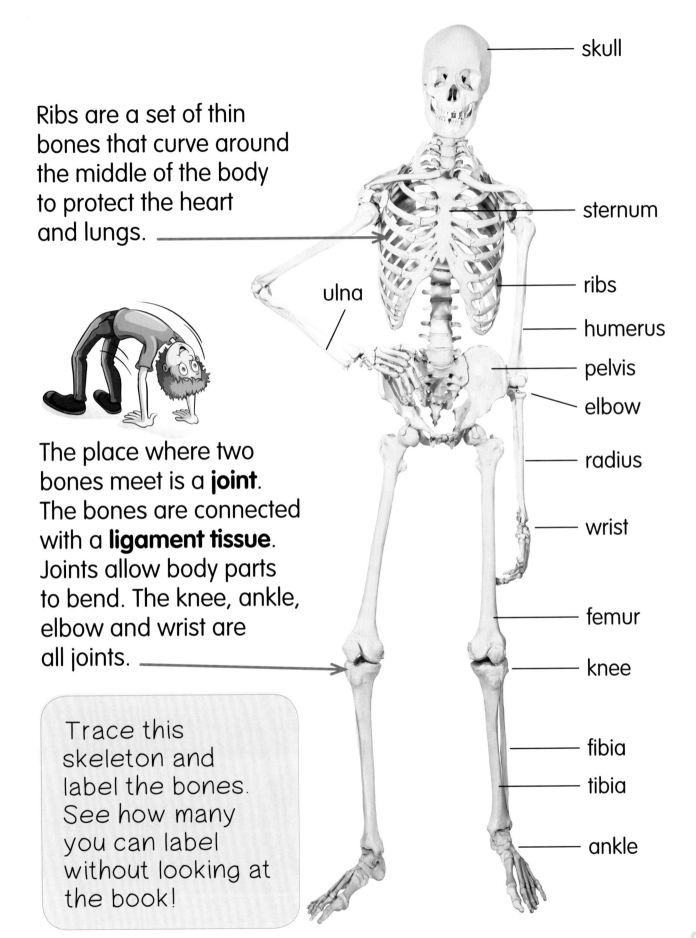

ulna

skull

sternum

ribs

humerus

pelvis

elbow

radius

wrist

femur

knee

fibia

tibia

ankle

Muscles

Muscles are fleshy tissues in the body that help us move. They are attached to bones by stretchy **tendons** (a bit like rubber bands).

Muscles work together so we can walk, kick or do any movement. We even use muscles to breath!

Keywords muscle tendon tissue

When using or squeezing a muscle, it **contracts** and gets shorter, pulling on the bone.

Muscles work in pairs to move a joint. While one muscle contracts and gets shorter, the other relaxes and becomes longer.

muscles

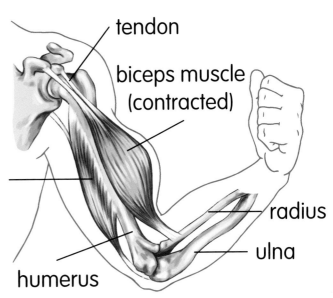

tendon

biceps muscle (contracted)

triceps muscle (relaxed)

radius

ulna

humerus

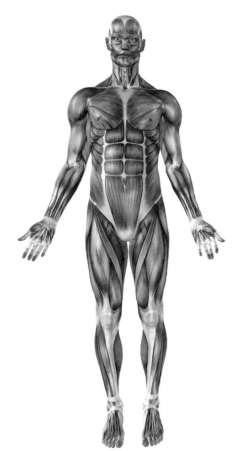

There are more than 600 muscles in the human body.

A lot of muscle movement is **voluntary**. Some muscle movement is involuntary, meaning it happens without the person even thinking about it. One example is your beating heart.

Blinking is also involuntary – how long can you not blink?

How muscles work

Make a moveable model arm to see how muscles contract and relax.

You will need:

- 2 kitchen paper tubes (bones)
- 2 long balloons (muscles)
- scissors
- pen or pencil
- pipe cleaner
- rubber band

rubber band

pipe cleaner

tubes

long balloon

Step 1: Make the bones. One tube will be the humerus. For the forearm, cut the second tube lengthways. Tape up each length to form the thinner radius and ulna. Label all three bones.

cut second tube lengthways

label bones

Step 2: Ask a grown-up to help you cut two holes through the bottom of the humerus; push through the pipe cleaner through both holes.

Step 3: Cut holes through the top of the radius and ulna. Then attach all the bones by pushing the pipe cleaner through each of these thinner bones and fold over the ends.

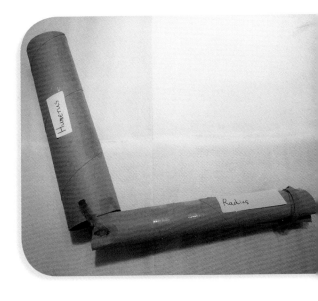

arm bones attached

Step 4: Wrap a rubber band around the bottom of the forearm bones, to act as a wrist.

Step 5: Now make the muscles. Blow up each balloon but only about halfway full. Squeeze the air to the centre, leaving long ends. Tie each end of the balloons to the bones; one for the biceps and the other for the triceps.

Your arm model is complete!

red biceps, blue triceps

Demonstrate how muscles work by bending the arm: the biceps (red balloon) will be squeezed and contract, leaving the triceps (blue balloon) flat and relaxed. Straighten the arm and see how the red biceps muscle stretches out.

The digestive system

We need energy to stay well and alive. Each part of the body needs energy to work properly. Where do we get this energy from? The answer: food! Let's find out what happens inside the body when we eat!

The body has a clever design of organs that work together to **process** food – this is digestion.

Keywords acid bloodstream digestion energy

The digestive system breaks down food so it can be **absorbed** into the bloodstream and spread energy and nutrients throughout the body.

The digestive system starts with the mouth and eating food.

We use our teeth to chew food into smaller pieces which are mixed with **saliva**. Chewed, moist food is easier to swallow.

The digestive system (continued)

What happens next?

After chewing and swallowing it, food moves down the **oesophagus** and into the stomach.

Here, **acid** breaks down the food into smaller particles.

swallowed food passes down the oesophagus

stomach acid helps digest food

stomach

Where does it go after that?

The broken-down food then travels into the small **intestine**, where nutrients in the food are absorbed into the bloodstream that flows around the body. It has a long way to go – an adult's small intestine can be over 7 metres long!

The remaining food keeps travelling through to the large intestine, where excess water is removed.

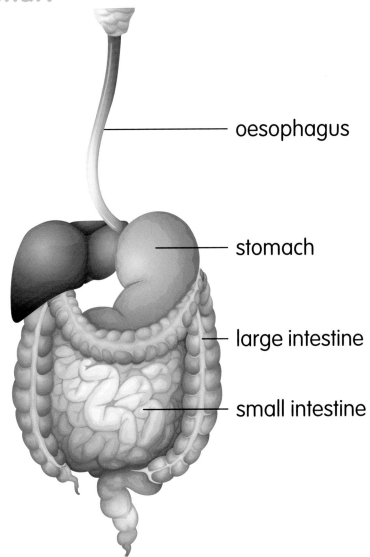

oesophagus

stomach

large intestine

small intestine

The leftover digested food, no longer of use to the body, comes out as waste!

Measuring the small intestine

The small intestine is a very long organ. A child's small intestine, if you stretched it all out, measures about 6 metres long. It is also about two and half centimetres in **diameter** (similar to a garden hose).

Let's put those facts to the test and find out how long our small intestine really looks!

You will need:

- garden hose
- tape measure
- a partner

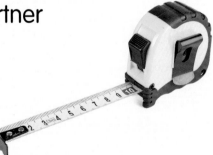

tape measure

garden hose

Step 1: Grab your hose and find space outside to stretch it out completely.

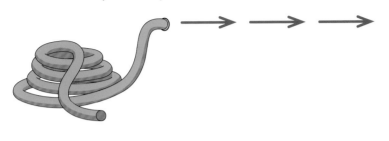

stretched-out hose

Step 2: Put the start of the tape measure at one end of the hose; ask your partner to hold it tightly in place.

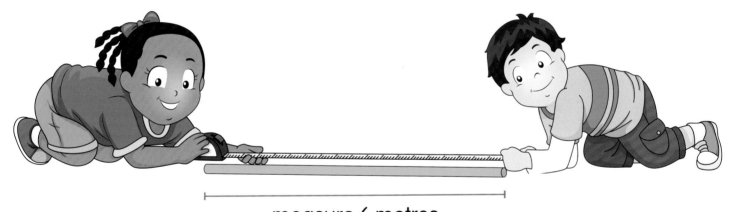

measure 6 metres

Step 3: Stretch out the tape measure along the hose to measure 6 metres. You may need to measure in two sections if the tape measure isn't long enough.

Now fold up the hose as tightly as possible and hold it front of you.

That's quite a lot of 'intestine' to fit inside your tummy!

Food and nutrients

To stay alive and grow, have energy and repair itself, the body needs food. Unlike plants, the human body cannot make its own food. We need to eat plenty of healthy foods. This means eating foods that contain **nutrients**.

Nutrients include vitamins such as A and C, as well as minerals, like iron and calcium.

strawberries – high in vitamin C

milk – high in calcium

red meat and spinach – high in iron

Keywords carbohydrates fats nutrient protein

The three main groups of nutrients in food are protein, carbohydrates and fats.

Look at the pictures on the right. Which triangle of foods belongs to which group?

Some people choose to **exclude** certain foods from their diet. Vegetarians do not eat meat or fish. Vegans do not eat meat, fish or any other animal product (such as butter). The vegan burger shown left is made with buckwheat instead of meat.

Vegetarians and vegans eat many different vegetables, fruits, grains, **legumes**, nuts and seeds to ensure they get enough nutrients.

Foods give energy to the heart, arms and legs, like fuel in a car. What is another part of the body that needs fuel to help it function properly? (Hint: you use it a lot during a test!)

Making a meal planner

Make a list of healthy foods that fit into the food groups below to make a meal planner. You can create one for breakfast, lunch and dinner for a single day, or several for a whole week of meals!

Carbohydrates
vegetables, fruit and grain-based foods such as bread, pasta and rice

Protein
meat, fish, eggs

Fats
dairy foods such as milk, cheese, yogurt

Note: some foods belong to more than one group.

Find pictures of your food choices online and print them out. Cut them up and glue them into a collage based on the template below. Each space shows how much of each food group we should eat compared to the others. Which foods should we eat most?

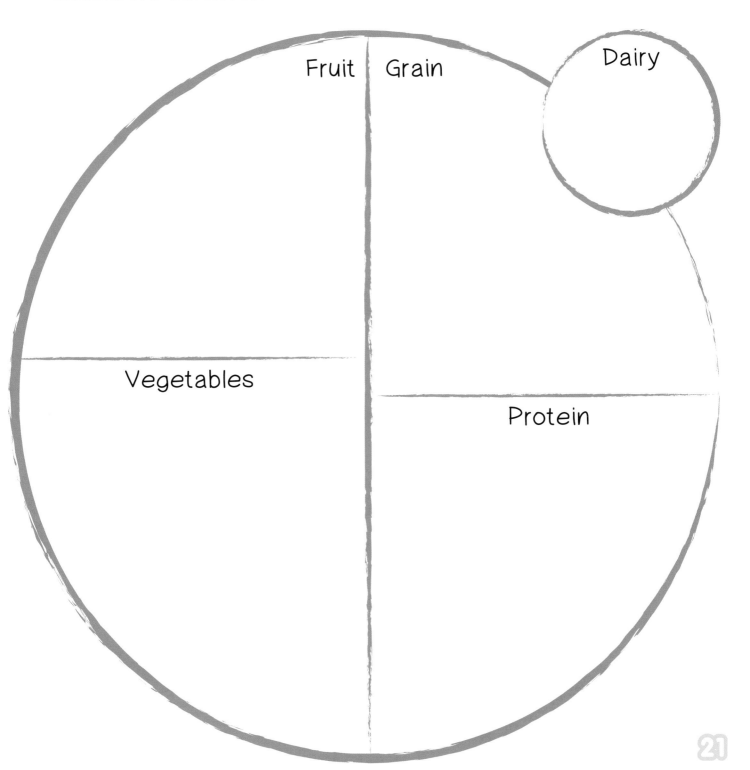

All about teeth

As babies, humans slowly grow their first set of teeth – known as milk teeth. Adult teeth start to push through around age 6 (Hello, Tooth Fairy!) Up to 32 adult teeth may develop. Each type of tooth is made for a particular job when eating.

There are four different types of teeth:

incisors that help you to bite food

canines for tearing food

molars and **pre-molars** that crush and grind food

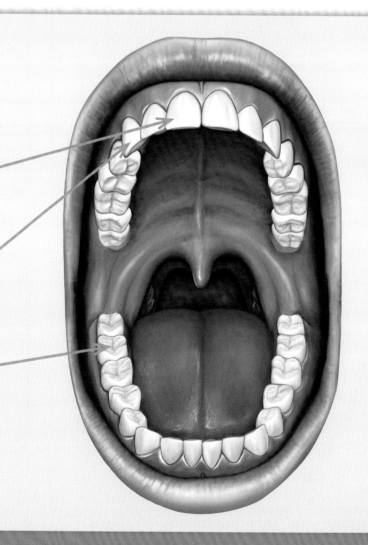

Keywords canine incisor molar

Adult teeth cannot be replaced naturally, so we need to look after them. Keep your teeth clean by brushing for at least two minutes, twice day.

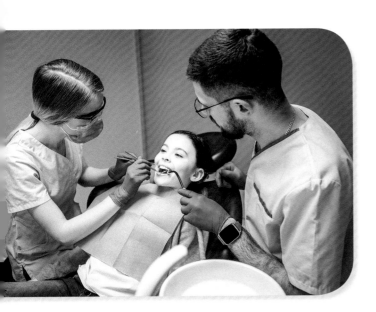

Eating the right foods and visiting the dentist **regularly** will also help to keep teeth and gums healthy.

Fun fact:

Before toothpaste was invented in the 1850s, people cleaned their teeth with chalk, charcoal and lemon juice!

Sugary foods and drinks can **rot** teeth and create a hole called a cavity.

Acid in fruit juice can wear away enamel, the teeth's protective coating.

Tooth decay

Sugar and food colouring can have a big effect on our teeth. This experiment tests what sugar and other substances can do to teeth. As we wouldn't want to test for decay on ourselves, the experiment uses eggs. Egg shell is similar to tooth enamel.

You will need:

- eggs
- water
- coloured, fizzy, flavoured drink
- vinegar
- toothpaste
- 4 small bowls

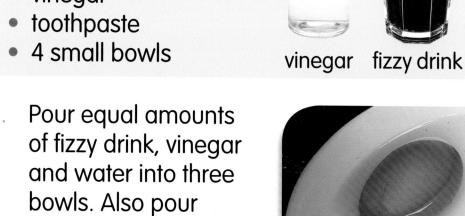

eggs

vinegar   fizzy drink   water

1. Pour equal amounts of fizzy drink, vinegar and water into three bowls. Also pour fizzy drink into the fourth bowl.

2. Add an egg to the bowls of vinegar, water and one fizzy drink. Cover the fourth egg with toothpaste and add it to the second bowl of fizzy drink. Leave the bowls for three days.

3. Then remove all the eggs. Rinse the egg from the vinegar bowl and rub it gently. What happens?

4. Is there any change to the egg from the water bowl?

5. How does the egg (without toothpaste) from the fizzy drink look?

6. Wipe off the toothpaste from the fourth egg.
How does that one look?

THE RESULTS

Egg from the vinegar bowl:

The egg shell should start to come off. Acid in the vinegar dissolves the shell, leaving just the slippery membrane covering behind.

This is similar to what happens when we eat sugary foods. Over time, bacteria in the mouth breaks down the sugar into acid which eats away at the protective enamel on the teeth.

Egg from the water bowl:

There should be no change.

Egg (without toothpaste) from the fizzy drink bowl:

It should be stained in a colour similar to the drink.

Fizzy coloured drinks contain sugar and ingredients that can stain the teeth.

Egg (with toothpaste) from the second fizzy drink bowl:

It should be less stained than the egg from the first fizzy drink as the toothpaste would have protected the shell from the staining ingredients.

Create a chart recording your experiment. Were the results as you expected?

	Egg in vinegar	Egg in water	Egg in fizzy drink	Toothpaste egg in fizzy drink
Prediction of what will happen:				
How the eggs look after 3 days:				

Comprehension check

1. What do we call the collection of bones in the body?

2. What are the set of thin bones that curve around the middle of the body?

3. What do we call the place where two bones meet?

4. What are the three long bones in the arm called?

5. When chewing food, what is it mixed with to help swallowing?

6. After food moves down through the oesophagus, where does it go next?

7. What are the three main food groups?

8. Which word describes someone who does not eat any animal products?

9. How many times a day must we brush our teeth?

10. What is the name for a hole in a tooth caused by eating sugary foods?

Turn to page 32 to mark your answers.

Vocabulary check

Fill in the blanks to complete these body facts:

1. For the human body to work properly, it needs energy and n _ _ _ _ _ _ _ _ .

2. M _ _ _ _ _ _ are fleshy tissues in the body that help us move.

3. When using or squeezing a muscle, it c _ _ _ _ _ _ _ _ _ and gets shorter, pulling on the bone.

4. In the body there are more than
   a) 25 bones
   b) 200 bones
   c) 1000 bones

5. From where does the human body get energy?

6. The processing of food through the body is d _ _ _ _ _ _ _ _ .

7. The digestive system breaks down food so it can be absorbed into the b _ _ _ _ _ _ _ _ _ and spread energy and nutrients throughout the body.

8. An adult's small i _ _ _ _ _ _ _ _ can be over 7 metres long.

9. A v _ _ _ _ _ _ _ _ _ does not eat meat or fish.

10. Slightly pointy teeth built for tearing food are called c _ _ _ _ _ _ _ .

Turn to page 32 to mark your answers.

Glossary

Definitions relate to the context of word usage in this book.

absorb – to take in or soak up

acid – a fluid in the stomach that helps to break down food

bloodstream – the blood that moves around the body of a living thing

bone – the hard tissue that forms the skeleton of a human or other animal

brain – the organ inside the skull that control's body movements and activities; where thoughts, memories and feelings come from

contract – to squeeze or use a muscle

demonstrate – to explain or describe

diameter – the width of a circle, cylinder or sphere

digestion – the processing and journey of food through the body

enable – to allow something to happen

energy – the power to make something work

exclude – to leave out

function – to work or perform fully

healthy – being well and fit; something that is good for you

intestine – the long tube that digested food travels through from the stomach

joint – the place where two bones meet and are connected by a ligament

legume – a plant that grows its seeds and fruit in a pod; beans and peas are legumes

ligament – a tissue connecting two bones to form a joint

muscle – soft parts, or tissues, of the body that allow movement

nutrient – a part of food that helps living things to live and grow

oesophagus – the tube that carries food from the mouth to the stomach

organ – a soft part of the body that does a job

perform – to do

process – a series of action to produce something or achieve a goal

recover – to get better from illness or injury

regularly – something that happens at evenly spaced periods of time

repair – to fix something that is damaged

rib – one of the bones that curve around the middle of the body and protect the heart and lungs

saliva – a liquid produced in the mouth to help the swallowing of food

sensory – something that includes use of the senses

shade – the amount of darkness in a colour

skeleton – the collection of bones in the body

skull – the bones in the head and face that protect the brain

stomach – the organ in the body that starts to digest swallowed food and then sends it to the small intestine

tendon – a stretchy tissue that attaches muscle to bone

voluntary – something done by choice

Index

Quiz answers

Comprehension check, page 28
1. skeleton 2. ribs 3. joint 4. humerus, radius and ulna 5. saliva
6. stomach 7. protein, carbohydrates and fats 8. vegan
9. at least twice 10. cavity

Vocabulary check, page 29
1. nutrients 2. muscles 3. contracts 4. b) more than 200 bones 5. food
6. digestion 7. bloodstream 8. intestine 9. vegetarian 10. canines

Photo credits

Shutterstock.com: Cover: Samuel Borges Photography; pp 1–2: GraphicsRF, yatate; pp 4–5: Monkey Business Images, bitt24, GraphicsRF, Lyudmyla Kharlamova; pp 6–7: Duda Vasilii, Philipp Nicolai, BlueRingMedia; pp 8–9: Martin Valigursky, Iulian Valentin, ANATOMIA3D, stihii; pp 10–11: Feng Yu, Alimag, timquo, KAMONRAT; pp 12–13: New Africa, BlueRingMedia, Glayan, Lorelyn Medina, pp 14–15: BlueRingMedia (x3), Kakigori Studio, Lorelyn Medina; pp 16–17: Andrew Angelov, eurobanks, Lorelyn Medina (x2), Robles Designery, Seregam; pp 18–19: Tim UR, baibaz, New Africa, David Fedulov, Valentyn Volkov, Polina Yanchuk; pp 20–21: Double Brain, Roman Samborskyi; pp 22–23: Andrea Danti, sutham, Estrada Anton, Jacky Brown; pp 24–25: Lorelyn Medina, wowow, studiovin, Luis Molinero, nelik, focal point, GraphicsRF; pp 26–27: Lorelyn Medina, Kastoluza, anmbph, Andrii Bezvershenko; pp 28–29: GraphicsRF, pp 30–32:GraphicsRF, Olkita, Lorelyn Medina, Teguh Mujiono

Author's photo: pp 10–11, pp 24–26: Nichola Tyrrell